Finding Francie

a memoir

Frances Pauline Morse

HighTide
Publications, Inc.

High Tide Publications, Inc.
1000 Bland Point
Deltaville, Virginia 23043
www.hightidepublications.com

Quantity sales. Special discounts are available on quantity purchases by corporations, associations, and others. For details, contact the "Special Sales Department" at the address above.

ISBN: 978-1-945990-81-6 (High Tide Publications, Inc.)

First Edition: March 28, 2017

BISAC: BIO026000 biography & autobiography/Personal Memoirs

Forward

The author of these stories is Frances P. Morse (Francie) born in 1943 – the first of Warren and Lucile Gille's six children. Francie and I have been married since 1967. Feel free to calculate how many years that's been. I still do.

Get ready for an adventure. I take some credit. As you will see shortly after college, I was headed to medical school in Chicago and shared with Francie that even if she moved to Chicago she might not see me for two years. Apparently, that was enough of a spark to ignite an odyssey that circled the globe. Fortunately, when it was all said and done, we "found" each other once again. And yes, I did finish medical school.

Once you have read a few of the stories you will understand the title of this book. The use of language is truly engaging and unpretentious, inviting us all into her heart – compassionate, sensitive, colorful, humorous. That's Francie. Enjoy!

Michael Morse

Contents

Frances P. Gille

1965

In the Beginning

It was the year 1965, the summer after my senior year in college. My college roommate Barbie and I had both graduated with teaching degrees. In the spring of our senior year, Barbie applied for teaching positions, according to my parents, the responsible thing to do. She was offered a job to teach third grade at an elementary school in Simi Valley, California. I, on the other hand, did not apply. You might say I was ambivalent about teaching and somewhat fearful that I might be typecast as a teacher the rest of my life. I wanted to be the "unsinkable Molly Brown" and "see all there was to see." I was an English major, but my father insisted that I also get a teaching degree so that I could get a job and be financially self-sustaining once I graduated.

Barbie, my parents, and my boyfriend Mike all had suggestions for me. Barbie wanted me to move to California, get a job, and share an apartment with her. Mike, who was about to begin his first year of medical school in Chicago, proposed that I move back home with my parents in Kansas City. Then every two months or so I could take the train to Chicago to see him. He said, "If you were in Chicago, you'd be a distraction." He was a bit anxious about medical school, and needed to focus his first year. Having grown up in the Great Depression and realizing that there were five additional candidates for college, my parents were understandably concerned that I find gainful employment. My father was very vocal on the matter.

It wasn't until the middle of August after my summer job as a camp counselor ended that I finally made a decision. Moving back home seemed like a waste of my newfound freedom. So, I sat down and wrote Barbie a letter saying that I was coming to California. I was taking the big leap and buying a one-way train ticket to Los Angeles! I sent the letter off post haste to Barbie's home address in Wisconsin. I was off on an adventure. As it turned out, it was more than I had reckoned for.

Traveling by train across country has some real advantages. It gave me time to reflect. I was on a journey to find myself and it felt both freeing and a little frightening as I faced the unknown. The Rocky Mountains in the fall were majestic with snowcapped peaks and golden aspen. It was snowing in Boulder, Colorado. I was sensitive to the cold since I was wearing sandals and an unlined wind breaker through rapidly melting snow flurries.

I reached Los Angeles, and Barbie was there to pick me up. It was early evening but still very warm outside, a welcome contrast to Colorado. Barbie seemed glad to see me but was rather pensive. When we headed home to her apartment in Canoga Park, a new suburb of Los Angeles, she spilled the beans. "I didn't realize that you had decided to come to California until a few days ago when I received your letter. Mom forwarded it to me," she explained. "You probably don't know that school started here about three weeks ago. I moved to California mid-August for teacher orientation and met another new teacher who was looking for a roommate. We rented a small, one-bedroom apartment. As you will see, there is no room for a third person." I took a big gulp. She said I was welcome to sleep on the couch in the living room until I could get an apartment of my own. "Ouch!" I didn't have a job and I didn't have a car. I only had about $200 in the bank and that wasn't enough.

The next several days were a scramble. I went out on foot looking for a job, and for public transportation. Canoga Park in the 1960s was still rural with vacant lots and an occasional strip mall—not many businesses besides a grocery store, a cleaner, barber shop and a travel agency. Only the grocery store was hiring. How did I feel about becoming a bag lady? The answer: *Not so good*. I might have been able to work myself up to a cashier position in a year or so. Four years of tuition at a private college to become a bag lady. I could do better than that.

After a full day of pounding the pavement, I realized that the employment opportunities were in the city. The nearest public transit was five miles from Barbie's apartment. Without a car, it seemed impossible. What to do? It seemed like I was at a dead end. One obvious option was to buy a return ticket home to Kansas City. I knew I would never hear the end of that. Then a bright idea occurred to me. Why not keep going west to Hawaii? A sorority sister from my college was Japanese. Her family lived on Maui. She was one year behind me in school, but was in Honolulu for the semester taking a Hawaiian history class so that after graduation she could return to Hawaii and teach. I wrote Geri Hamii a letter explaining my idea and waited for her reply.

In the meantime, I telephoned my parents and told them about my newest plan to buy a one way ticket to Honolulu. My parents were not pleased. In fact, my mother cautioned my dad about cussing over the phone line. And then she added, "Your boyfriend Mike called. He said he had lost our phone number when he moved to medical school and just found it." I took his medical school address and vowed I would write him a letter once I knew exactly what I was doing.

The response came from Geri in less than two weeks. She was delighted that I was interested in coming to Honolulu and said, "Come ahead." That was all the encouragement I needed. I bought a one-way ticket from LAX, repacked my little suitcase, and was soon winging my way across the Pacific Ocean.

It was a warm, cloudy afternoon as we entered the air-traffic pattern at the Honolulu International Airport. As we descended through the clouds, I could see the lush green mountainside and blue waters of the Pacific. When we landed, many of the passengers were greeted by local people with flower leis. A slight gust of wind, warm and moist, gently brushed my cheek as I stepped off the plane. "I think I'm going to like this place," I said to no one in particular.

The airport shuttle dropped me in Waikiki. As I walked down the main boulevard, it began to rain. The locals in their muumuus stepped under store awnings, reached down and slipped off their shoes and put them in their shopping bags. *Yes*, I thought, *I'm definitely going to like this place!*

I am Blessed

I called Geri and told her I had arrived in Honolulu. It was wonderfully reassuring to hear her voice on the other end of the phone line. She said she was going to pick me up and bring me to the Tanner's home where she was working as an au pair caring for their six children. When Geri was not attending classes, she was babysitting, doing light housework, and running errands in exchange for room, board and a small salary. Dr. and Mrs. Tanner insisted that I stay with them until I found appropriate housing which I greatly appreciated.

The following afternoon Geri drove me to the student services office at the University of Hawaii to look at the housing board. Almost immediately I spied the following notice: Tutor needed for two elementary aged Japanese-American boys in exchange for room and board. *This might be just the ticket*, I thought to myself. Geri and I made an appointment to meet with the mother and her sons later that afternoon.

The Masuda family lived in a modest three-bedroom, one bath home in an older area of Honolulu not far from the public bus route. Mr. Masuda was a building contractor who was gone much of the time. They had two sons: Coyne (4th grade) and Calvin (3rd grade) plus a five-year-old daughter named Fay. Coyne was struggling in school, had difficulty staying on task, and had some disruptive behavioral issues in the classroom. If his grades and behavior did not improve, he would not pass the fourth grade. In hindsight, Coyne was probably learning disabled, but as a *green-behind-the-ears* teacher, I didn't recognize that. Calvin, about ten months younger, was a bright, inquisitive third grader who was very interested in knowing what I would be doing with them. It was obvious that Mrs. Masuda had purposely made the decision to have both boys tutored not to single out Coyne as the troubled child. If I accepted the position, I would be tutoring the boys for two hours four nights a week.

"I will show you the room," Mrs. Masuda said as she led me through the kitchen and out the back door to a tool shed in the backyard. It had one small screened window for ventilation, a cot, a small chest of drawers, a chair, and several hooks for clothing or towels. It was modest by any standard. As we stepped into the tiny, low ceilinged space, a large roach, the biggest I had ever seen, scampered across the concrete floor. Mrs. Masuda quickly stomped on it reassuring me that, "they don't bite."

I made a quick decision as Geri and I were leaving the house. I believed that I could really help Coyne and that I would enjoy working with Calvin with his impish grin. Yes, I'd take the job. The room and board was an answer to my prayer. And, best of all, I could move in immediately.

With my room and board taken care of, I could relax a bit. Here I was in beautiful Hawaii blessed to have a job. I was making it on my own. My only need was a part-time position making enough money to pay for other living expenses. So, the following day, which was Friday, I took the local bus to the administrative offices of the Board of Education to apply for a substitute teaching position. It was a sunny early fall day. The palm trees were gently swaying in the breeze. Red, purple, and pink bougainvillea and yellow plumaria colored the landscape.

The bus driver signaled me at my stop. I wanted to leap from the bus like Julie Andrews did in *The Sound of Music* singing *I've got confidence in me*. Of course I didn't. As I read the application, and began filling it out, I realized by substituting just one day a week, I would be financially solvent. I handed in the completed application and was then called into the administrator's office for an interview. An amazing thing happened. I was offered a full-time teaching position at Kalakaua Intermediate School in Kalihi, a very old blue collar neighborhood in Honolulu. The school had lost a teacher about ten days before, and they were desperately looking for a permanent replacement to teach English and social studies of the Hawaiian Islands. That might be a challenge! She said she could offer me a position subject to the principal's approval. "You start Monday morning," was ringing in my ears. My guardian angel was working overtime.

Toto, We're Not in Kansas Anymore

Teaching in Honolulu was a far cry from student teaching in Galesburg, Illinois. This was the first time that I was part of a racial minority. At least 90% of the students and faculty were Japanese, Chinese, Filipino, Hawaiian, mixed, or another ethnicity.

An additional challenge was that I was not only teaching seventh grade English but also the history of the Hawaiian Islands. This was going to be interesting. Basically my knowledge of Hawaiian history was limited to the information I had read in a travel brochure.

The middle school was in a very poor section of Honolulu where unemployment was high and school dropouts were numerous. It was less than a block from one of the roughest high schools in Honolulu. Unfortunately, this was also the location of my bus stop to commute to and from home. Walking through the hordes of teens smoking cigarettes and loudly talking among themselves was rather intimidating. "Keep moving" I said to myself. "Just get on the bus." Once safely on the bus, it was still a long ride with many stops before I was home.

It was a true blessing when one of the Japanese teachers asked me where I was living. When we discovered our homes were in the same area, he offered to pick me up in the morning and bring me home in the afternoon. In exchange, I would reimburse him the cost of my bus fare. It is what I called a win-win situation. The original school building was built shortly after World War I. It had a high ceiling which transformed it into an echoing relic. As the school population grew, mobile classrooms were added. My classroom was in one of those out buildings far from the main office. Basically, I was on my own which made me rather anxious. On that first Monday, I was given a set of textbooks for my classes and a key to my classroom with instructions that my homeroom students were responsible for sweeping and mopping the room at the end of each day under my supervision. I had 36 desks tightly crammed into this little space. To make matters worse, my fourth period was a remedial 9th-grade English class. It had 42 students enrolled in it. If all the students attended class, six students would be sitting on the floor. Any self-respecting fire marshal would have shut us down in a heartbeat.

The second major issue was at least half of the students were repeating the class for the second time. The English textbook was boring and above their reading level. One student even threw his textbook out the open window. I needed to revise the curriculum and make the reading material deal with more relevant issues. Several things came to mind: filling out a job application; preparing for a job interview; using good grammar instead of Pidgin English.[1]

---

1   **Hawaiian Pidgin English, Hawaiian Creole English, HCE,** or locally known as simply **Pidgin,** is a creole language based in part on English, spoken by many residents of Hawaii. Although English and Hawaiian are the co-official languages of the state of Hawaii,[3] Hawaiian Pidgin is used by many Hawaii residents in everyday casual conversation and is often used in advertising targeted toward locals in Hawaii. In the Hawaiian language, Hawaiian Creole English is called "'ōlelo pa'i 'ai", which literally means "pounding-taro language".

Despite its name, Hawaiian Pidgin is not a pidgin, but rather a full-fledged, nativized, and demographically stable natural language. It did, however, evolve from various real pidgins spoken between ethnic groups in Hawaii.

As it turned out, I need not have worried about the enrollment. Several students transferred out of the classes, and four boys were absent the first few days. I finally asked the other students if anyone knew where the boys were. Someone said, "Hey teacher, they be skippin." I gathered myself to my full five feet, two inches and said, "Give them a message from me. They need to be in class tomorrow or they will be in big trouble!" That should scare them....well, maybe not.

The next day I stood at the door of my classroom fourth period, holding my breath. As I was about to give up hope I breathed a sigh of relief when four slick-looking, dark haired dudes dressed in black tees and baggy black pants sauntered up to me. They looked like they had just stepped out of West Side Story.

"Hey you young haole teechar?" asked the apparent leader of the pack.

"Take a seat, gentlemen. I'll speak with you after class."

As a consequence for skipping, I told them they would need to report to my classroom after school the next day to sweep and mop, relieving my homeroom students from that responsibility. I was taking a big gamble. What if they didn't come? What then? That was another learning moment for me. Don't make consequences that you can't enforce.

The next day, just as I was giving up hope, in they walked. They picked up the broom, mops, and bucket and, before long, the classroom was clean. While we were waiting for the floor to dry, I took out my camera and began taking photos of them. They rose to the occasion by "sword fighting" with the mops, and posing as a bucket brigade. I promised to make them copies of those photos when I got them developed. They were having fun.

Skipping was rarely a problem from that point on.

In the Minority

For the first time in my life I was in the minority. I was the only Caucasian on faculty and I was, by far, the youngest faculty member. Most of the teachers were Japanese or Chinese. They ate their lunch in the teachers' lounge across campus in the main building. I longed for some adult contact, so I began walking over to the main building at lunchtime. I noticed when I entered the lounge, they would lower their voices or begin talking in their native language. I made a few feeble attempts to introduce myself and to start a conversation with little response. I was alone in a crowded room.

After a week of this, I was beginning to think I would be better off just eating alone in my classroom. And then it happened. A kindly older Japanese gentleman came over to my table and asked if he could join me. This happened for several days and soon other teachers were inviting me to join their lunch group. I promised myself I would be much more sensitive and inclusive of minorities in the future.

I'm Reviewing the Situation

It was almost Thanksgiving. I was pleased that the Masuda boys were doing better in school. Coyne's behavior in class and his grades had improved though it was clear that school would never be his strong suit. Calvin, on the other hand, was doing excellent work - involved in what he was learning.

I was also getting to know my students. I made it a point to go in early and to stay late after school since many of my kids would wander in to chat about their problems. I learned that some of the most important aspects of teaching are building trusting relationships with one's students, being a good listener, and laughing together. To me, that personal sharing time seemed far more important than learning sentence structure and punctuation. For instance, one bright seventh grader named Tiave was chronically late to my class. When I asked him why, he said he had to get his shoes from his brother. The middle school had a policy that all students must wear shoes in class. Tiave was one of nine children and his family didn't have the money to buy all the kids shoes, so he shared with his brother. I told Tiave to forget the shoes. It was much more important for him to be in class on time and not miss part of the lesson.

My week days were extremely busy. I was teaching all day, tutoring in the evening, correcting papers, and making lesson plans before bed and repeating the process the next day. Saturday was my R and R day - doing laundry, shopping, napping, writing letters to my family, and to Mike. I looked forward to letters from home- especially from Mike. He was doing well in medical school and excited about his clinical rotations. He had such a heart for helping people.

Geri was such a good friend and life line. Often, on Saturday afternoon or evening, we "hung out" together. She introduced me to several other University of Hawaii students. I quietly dreaded the fact that she would be returning to Knox College in 90 days. Ironically, one of the students that she introduced me to, Barbara Dunn, had graduated from Knox College as part of my graduating class of two hundred. She was at the University of Hawaii getting her master's degree in library science. Barbara lived in a high rise with another student. Because the rent was expensive, they were looking for a third roommate. At that moment, I was happily settled...or so I thought. Life was about to throw me another curve ball, however.

I was excited about flying home for Christmas break, and I must admit I was a little homesick for Mike and my family. Every time I heard *I'll be Home for Christmas* I got teary eyed. It was a wonderful surprise to see Mike at the Kansas City airport welcoming me home! Needless to say, he was just what the doctor ordered.

When I arrived back in Honolulu after Christmas, Mrs. Masuda said she needed to talk to me. From the tone in her voice I could tell something serious had happened. Over the Christmas holiday they had sold their home and bought a new, larger home and would be moving to a gated community. She was about five months pregnant with their fourth child and needed the extra space. She also added that Mr. Masuda, fifteen years her senior, had a drinking problem which he was finally addressing. For her, the new baby and new house were new beginnings for the family. I could not have been happier for them. However, it did present a problem for me. I had a two-week notice to find another place to live.

I called Barbara Dunn and asked if they were still looking for a roommate. Barb said she had made the decision to move and was going to look at a room in a rooming house that was walking distance from the University of Hawaii. Would I like to come along? The rooming house was built above the Japanese family who owned the building. It had 5 bedrooms with two baths and a small kitchen. There was one bedroom for rent with 2 twin beds. The location worked beautifully for Barb and I thought "Why not?"

Big things were happening on my job front, too. The semester would be ending shortly and the principal at the middle school was pressing me to renew my teaching contract for the second semester. I was thinking that I would like to take a few courses at the University of Hawaii as an unclassified graduate student. I had to support myself, however. If I could get a job waitressing at one of the large hotels in the evening, I could take classes during the day and try to decide where I was going next. It was clear God had a plan and, bit by bit, He was sharing it with me.

The next day after school I took the bus down to the Royal Hawaiian Hotel, the grand old Pink Lady on Waikiki Beach. Back in the day, the hotel sat on the beach on a lovely, well-manicured green lawn. I marched into the elegant lobby and asked where the personnel office was. The desk clerk in his neatly pressed uniform looked at me over his horn-rimmed glasses and pointed out the door to a separate entrance in an adjacent building. After I completed the application, I was interviewed by a pudgy little forty-year-old man who seemed more interested in chatting about my personal life than my qualifications. He told me that waitress positions were usually filled by local people, not Caucasians from the mainland. He said he might be able to pull some strings and get me a job in the Surf Room, a formal dining room, but I would "owe him one." I wasn't quite sure what that meant, but it didn't sound good to me.

I started my waitressing job at the Royal Hawaiian Hotel the following week. It was very hard to say goodbye to my students. What I had learned from them was invaluable. Bottom line: I wasn't an English teacher at heart. I was much more interested in the emotional well-being of my students. As Mike and I wrote letters to one another about our experiences, it became evident that we both loved connecting with and helping others. We were both separately discovering who we were and what God intended for us to do. I was moving forward.

The Surf Room

The Surf Room at the Royal Hawaiian Hotel was a world apart from teaching at the middle school in Kalihi. The formal dining room bordering the beach had a 180—degree view of the Pacific Ocean. The tables were set with burgundy tablecloths and napkins and each table had a candle that glimmered in the twilight.

The waitresses arrived at 5:00 p.m. to set up the dining room. Everything had to be "perfect" by 6:00 p.m. when the first guests arrived. The French maître de, Jacque, impeccably dressed in a black tuxedo, began greeting and seating guests while the muumuu clad wait staff stood at their stations ready to serve every culinary need of our dinner guests. About 8:00 p.m. a small Hawaiian combo in aloha shirts arrived to serenade our guests with Hawaiian music. *Dreams Come True in Blue Hawaii* created a warm, romantic, nearly perfect evening.

Back in the kitchen, it was a different story. Waitresses scurried to and fro, submitting dinner orders to the two chefs, getting special requests, serving up salad, fetching aged wine, ice buckets, etc. To me, it was like a fire drill since I knew little about the dining room. My head was swimming with requests and special orders. Just as I thought

I was drowning and wouldn't come up for air, a waitress from my wait team named Alberta Choo graciously stepped in to help. Over the next few weeks, Alberta became my self-appointed mentor and friend and I missed her on her days off.

The dining room was divided into two service teams. I was on team B. I immediately noticed that all of the wait staff except for me were Chinese, Japanese, or Hawaiian women. Once again, I was in the minority. With the exception of Alberta, the other waitresses were cool and aloof. I gave myself a pep talk. I've been through this before. I can work though their resentment. Clearly, they feel that I am an outsider who has taken a job from one of their own. Hang in there, girl!

I was told the waitresses put their tips in a communal tip jar. The tips would be counted and divided after the dining room closed. I wasn't sure about the tip sharing but decided that it was their dining room and I needed to play by their rules. By the end of the evening, I had contributed more than $25.00 in tips—not bad for a first night's work. I was aching all over and could have slept standing up, but I had survived!

The next day when I arrived at work, I was handed a paper napkin with $5.50 in change as "my share" of the previous night's tips. I asked Alberta why my share was so small. She said, "Because you are in training." By the end of the week I was pulling my own weight and receiving a larger share of the tips. I often sat in the kitchen after the dining room closed eating a late supper and chatting with my fellow waitresses about work, family, and their pride in their jobs. I told them about Mike and my interest in social work. Somewhere in the person to person, woman to woman exchange they forgave me for being a young Caucasian on their turf.

A Line in the Sand

Then it happened. About a month into the job I was feeling pretty cocky. Work was going well. I was enjoying my courses at the University of Hawaii and thinking seriously about getting my master's degree.

That night, when I arrived at work, I was told that Team A was short a wait staff person so I would be filling in on the other side of the dining room for the evening. I knew the ropes. This was no big deal. Of course, I would rather be with my own team, but I could help out. By the time my shift ended, the tip jar was full.

I returned to my own team the following evening. As we were setting up, a Japanese waitress from Team A approached me with a paper napkin in her hand. I have a bad feeling about this. I thought to myself. Seven dollars in small coins. I should have seen this coming. Damn it! I was mad. I walked over to the Japanese waitress who had given me that fateful napkin. She was sorting silverware on a metal serving cart and I said, "If you can't give me my fair share of the tips, don't give me anything at all." With that I threw the napkin full of coins onto the metal cart. They made a terrible sound and splattered all over the floor as I walked away. All the wait staff paused and looked up. Several of the Japanese waitresses scurried over to pick up the coins. They were speaking Japanese now and I am sure it was not complimentary. Later that evening, a Japanese waitress from my team came as a good will ambassador from Team A and gave me a new paper napkin with $18.00 in it and a small apology. Needless to say, I was never asked to work on their side of the dining room again.

I learned to love these women and know some intimate details of their lives. I was particularly close to my friend Alberta. She was Chinese-Hawaiian, born and bred in Honolulu. She was surprisingly tall which I attributed to her Hawaiian heritage. Though she was only 37, she looked considerably older with permanent wrinkle lines in her face. Over time, I found out she was the mother of five and that her husband was a civilian employee for the army base. They lived in subsidized housing in Kalihi. (It was ironic to think that I could have had one of her kids in my classroom.) Because Hawaii is an expensive place to live, the family needed a second income to survive. So, several years ago she began working at the Royal Hawaiian Hotel. Her husband resented that she was gone so many nights a week. He refused to take care of the children, leaving that responsibility to her sixteen-year- old daughter who, in turn, resented both parents for making her the surrogate parent. I knew that some nights when Alberta returned home about 11:30 p.m., her husband was lying in wait for her and was verbally abusive. Her teenage daughter was now threating to run away from home, yet Alberta couldn't afford to quit her job. It was a vicious cycle. Her sad situation brought tears to my eyes.

When Alberta did not come to work for almost a week I became very concerned and called her. She said she had been in a car accident and hoped to be back soon. When Alberta returned she was very bruised, physically and emotionally. Though her body was healing, her spirit was not. She whispered that she felt so hopeless that she had thrown herself from a moving car in an effort to end it all. Fortunately, her injuries were not serious. I encouraged her to get counseling and helped her locate a community counseling service that had a sliding fee scale dependent on income. It took several weeks and some prodding to get her to go that first time to her appointment, but she really valued the professional support and reassurance that she was not alone.

Alberta asked me to talk with her teenage daughter—my first unofficial foray into social work. I got to know the Choo family well. At Easter Alberta invited me to their family luau: roast pig, chicken long rice, beer, ukulele music and all! Lots of uncles were playing music and drinking beer, lots of aunties were in the kitchen bringing out food and more food and sharing hugs. The best news was that Alberta transferred to the day shift and things got better at home.

Mike came to Hawaii for a visit during his spring break from medical school. It was wonderful to be with him and to share my island home and friends. We did some of the tourist activities like going to Pearl Harbor, Sea Life Park, and walking on the beach, but mostly we just enjoyed being together. This man was just stealing my heart. It was getting increasingly difficult to say good-bye.

On Mothers' Day, May, 1966, I received an early morning phone call. Much to my surprise, it was Mike, Geri Hamii, and our friend Ellie calling from Knox College. Mike had been there visiting fraternity brothers and decided to call. At the end of the conversation, Mike said he would really like me to come back to Chicago. Hawaii was too far away. Ellie and several friends who were graduating planned to rent an apartment together in the fall. Would I like to live with them? Mike missed me. My heart melted. I was ready to go home. I was finding Francie.

Plotting My Course

I tossed and turned that night thinking about Mike's request that I return to Chicago in the fall. I couldn't sleep. He wanted me to come home! My adrenalin was pumping. I was delighted and excited. Flying back to Chicago via Los Angeles seemed like a very anti-climactic ending to my nine—month adventure in Hawaii.

About midnight, I got an idea. Rather than flying east to Chicago, why not fly west and see part of the world that I had never seen before? The next day I went to a travel agency in downtown Honolulu to see if what I was plotting was even financially feasible. Together we traced the proposed route on a large wall map of the world. If I was willing to travel by cruise ship to Japan and Hong Kong, the ticket would be cheaper. So I plotted out my route: Honolulu to Japan, Hong Kong, Bangkok, Calcutta, Kathmandu, New Delhi, Baghdad, Damascus, Jerusalem, Tel Aviv, London and Chicago.

This was back in the days when airlines treated passengers like valued customers. When I could not make reasonable connections to my next flight, the airline would pay my hotel accommodations and meals. And, best of all, the ticket could be changed with no fee. I was elated!

The ticket was less than $1,200. I could afford it. Since it is always better to travel with a friend for safety sake, I spoke with several women including my roommate Barb. Everyone was either in school, or working, or could not afford it. They probably were thinking I was a nut case for planning this trip. Few women traveled alone in third world countries in those days. So, if I was going around the world, I'd be going alone. "Nothing ventured, nothing gained," as my mother used to say. And so I ventured out on my own to see the world.

Aloha

The Surf Room waitresses gave me a going away party after work one night at a local bar and grill during the week before I was to set sail for Yokohama, Japan. We were a raucous group, telling stories, laughing a lot, and probably drinking a little too much. They had an Aloha cake to wish me well. I found myself looking at each woman and my roommate Barb and remembering our first days together. I would miss them and forever be grateful for their friendship and love.

My ship sailed the evening of June 9, 1966, from the pier in Honolulu. The Royal Hawaiian band was on hand to serenade us with *The Hawaiian Wedding Song*. My friend Barb and Janet, a fellow waitress from the Surf Room stood on the dock gazed up at me.

I couldn't help but feel a twinge of sadness. I was closing an important chapter of my life and opening another. I had learned to cope in a different culture and to be financially independent. I threw my lei into the water as was the custom and whispered, "Aloha, Hawaii, I'll be back."

Around the World in Eighty Days

The cruise ship would be at sea for seven days. I needed time to rest and to reflect on my time in Hawaii. I also needed to prepare for the next leg of my journey. The weather was perfect; lots of sunshine, blue skies, and calm seas. There were several classes of cabins and two dining rooms.

I could only afford the *cheap seats*. Here I was in steerage- the bottom deck of the ship. Fortunately, I discovered that I was not prone to seasickness as those of us below were tossed about with choppy seas. I also ate my meals in the bowels of the ship at an assigned table with two seventeen-year-old girls, Jan (an American) and Mieko, who was Japanese. Jan's family had hosted Mieko for a year as a foreign exchange student in Ann Arbor, Michigan. Now Jan was returning to Japan with Mieko to spend a month with Mieko's Japanese family. These girls were the age of my sister, and I enjoyed their company. We explored the ship together and, over that week at sea, we became friends. The night before we docked at Yokohoma, Japan, Mieko asked me what I planned to do. I told her that I was going to the pearl diving area along the coast and then to Tokyo for a few days. Mieko said, "You must come and stay with my family when you get to Tokyo. This is my phone number," she insisted. I reminded Mieko that she was returning home with an American house guest already and that her parents had not seen her in almost a year. *Maybe another house guest was not a good idea.* "Call me" were Meiko's last words as they drove away.

The next morning the girls were picked up by Mieko's brother and a driver and were whisked off to Tokyo. I exchanged some dollars for Yen and bought a one-way ticket to Toba, a small seaside town in the pearl-diving district along the sea coast. There was a youth hostel where I would stay on the first night of my trip.

I didn't bargain for what was about to happen next.

The train trip took significantly longer than I anticipated. It was very dark when the train arrived at my stop. To make matters worse, it was pouring down rain. The little train station and platform were well lit when I stepped off the train. The station, however, was closed.

I was the only passenger who got off the train at this stop. That should have been a clue. I was greeted by hundreds of fiddler crabs scampering to and fro on the train platform. I looked out at the torrent of rain and darkness. What now? Where was the youth hostel? There was a small mom and pop store across the railroad tracks.

I headed across the track to see if anyone was around. I peered in the window, and could see lights in the back of the house. Two little children were playing on the floor nearby. The store front was dark – obviously closed for the day.

I knocked. No answer. "Yoo hoo?" I called out. A Japanese man came to the door. I must have been a sight, standing in the rain with my hair plastered to my head and my backpack on. It was not pretty. I managed to say the word "Youth Hostel" in Japanese. He pointed to a foot path and waved me on.

There were no street lights- probably because there were no streets. Periodically, I saw lights from small homes along the path. I didn't have the good sense to bring a flashlight or umbrella with me. Cold rain water trickled down my glasses, blurring my vision. *Am I going in the right direction?* I asked myself as I picked my way along.

I decided to stop at the next home along the way and ask again. A distinguished gentleman dressed in a kimono answered the door. Again, I asked for the student youth hostel. He pointed to the footpath. Then he signaled to me to wait a moment. He returned to the doorway wearing wooden clogs and carrying a flashlight and an umbrella. He stepped out in the rain, putting the large umbrella over both of us. We continued without conversation for another ten minutes or so. He stopped at the base of a large hill and pointed upward. I could see nothing but darkness.

Though we had barely been able to communicate, I trusted the kind and thoughtful man who stepped out in the rain and walked a mile with me. "A good Samaritan," I told myself. "Arigato," I said. (thank you in Japanese). He bowed slightly and disappeared into the darkness.

I began my climb up the steep hillside. I was cold and soaked to the skin and my backpack was getting heavier by the moment. As I reached the top of the hill, I was ecstatic to see the youth hostel with its lights still on. Now I prayed that there was a vacant bed where I could hang my hat for the night.

It was about 7:30 p.m. I had not eaten since early morning on the ship and I was getting hungrier by the moment. Though the dinner was over, the manager of the youth hostel took pity on me and brought me some soup and rice. I was very grateful.

My next goal was to get dry and warm. I decided to check out the bathroom facilities and was happy to not only find showers but also a large hot tub. I pulled off my wet clothes, slipped into a long tee shirt, grabbed my soap, towel, and tube of Prell shampoo, and headed for heaven.

No one else was in the bathroom, so I slipped into the hot tub and soaped up. Bubbles began foaming all over the tub as well as my plastic tube of Prell. Just as I was floating care free across the foamy hot tub, in walked three young Japanese girls who began bowing and making twittering noises. They immediately went to the showers, soaped up and rinsed off and got into the hot tub with me.

"Oh, so that's how you do it." I exclaimed. One of the girls handed me the Prell tube that had floated within her reach. Even though we all realized my faux pas, I bravely stepped out of the hot tub, lathered once again with soap and rinsed off under the cold shower. I was making a statement—see, you can teach a young American new tricks.

Meeting the Nakasones

I took the red-eye train to Tokyo the next evening and arrived about 7:30 in the morning. The streets of Tokyo were already teeming with cars, buses, taxis, bicycles, and traffic police all immersed in early morning smog. I stood on a crowded street corner looking at my map, and wondering how I would ever find a place to stay that I could afford. Two days in Japan and I was overwhelmed. *Pull it together, girl,* I told myself.

I remembered that on the cruise ship I had met a group of college coeds from California who also were going to Tokyo to study for one month. I had not spent much time with them on ship because they were part of the *party hardy* crowd on board, drinking and partying until the wee hours of the morning. I did connect with one of the friendlier girls. Her name was Linda and, like me, she was interested in a challenging adventure while in Tokyo. We had talked about the possibility of hiking Mt. Fuji together when I got to Tokyo. I had the name of her group and the name of their hotel in downtown Tokyo. So, ignoring the early hour, I found their hotel and went up to their room.

A blurry-eyed coed with pink rollers in her hair answered the door. It wasn't Linda!

Maybe I have the wrong room! Fortunately, Linda was in the room. *Whew.* I asked if I might make a local call to Mieko. I was relieved when the Japanese woman at the other end of the phone called Mieko. Mieko said that she had spoken with her parents about my visit to Tokyo, and her parents insisted I stay with them as their house guest. She told me to wait out front of the hotel in 45 minutes because she, Jan, and Mieko's brother Hirofumi would come and pick me up. What a blessing! In the meantime, Linda and I exchanged phone numbers and planned to talk in a day or two about our Mt Fuji trek.

Mieko, Jan and Hirofumi were a sight for sore eyes when they pulled up in a sleek black Mercedes Benz. I jumped into the back seat and we sped off through the congested streets of Tokyo, arriving in an upscale, exclusive neighborhood. The homes were large on very small lots. There was almost no yard. *Land must be very expensive*, I thought.

When we pulled up in front of the Nakasones' home, I noticed there were construction trucks in front. Mieko explained that her parents were adding a third story master suite to their home. I was getting the impression that this was not your average, middle-class Japanese family.

Mrs. Nakasone, a petite lady who spoke very little English, greeted us. Over the next few days it became clear that she was distressed because Mieko had adopted some new American ideas. Mieko told me that her parents were very old fashioned. They believed in arranged marriages. Mieko said that she preferred the American custom of selecting her own husband. I suggested that Mieko wait a while before sharing more new American ideas with her parents. Mieko nodded, acknowledging my suggestion.

That night Mr. Nakasone announced that he would be preparing a traditional Japanese stir fry called sukiyaki for dinner. The maid had chopped the meat and vegetables into neat, organized little piles. Mr. Nakasone made a grand entrance into the kitchen wearing a beautiful silk kimono with an obi sash at his waist. *This dark haired, stately gentleman is very handsome,* I thought as he picked up the cooking chopsticks, much like a conductor picks up a baton, and began to cook.

The doorbell rang, and the maid hurried to answer it. She soon returned with a message for Mr. Nakasone. He handed the cooking chopsticks to the maid, apologized for the interruption, and went down to meet the visitor. Being the curious person that I am, I asked Mieko what was going on? She said that a reporter from the newspaper had come to interview her father about a project he was working on. I then asked the next obvious question. "What does your father do for a living?" "Oh, he works for the government in the Office of Transportation and Travel," she said matter-of-factly.

On another evening after dinner, Mr. Nakasone arranged to have his driver and his male secretary take us three girls to a religious festival at one of the shrines because he was tied up in an important meeting. Who was this man, anyway?

Climbing Mt. Fuji

Approximately 70 per cent of Japan is mountainous, so farmable land is scarce. Often on my trip I saw terraced hillsides with every inch planted with rice paddies to meet the needs of the large population. The tallest mountain peak in Japan is Mt. Fuji; the summit is 12,385 feet tall. It is still classified as an active volcano, even though its last eruption was in 1707. *Fodor's Guidebook on Japan* said, "Mt. Fuji greets the hikers who arrive at the summit just before dawn with the *Honorable Coming of the Light.* The reflection of its light shimmers across the sky just before the sun first appears, giving the extra ordinary sunrise a mystical feel." That sounded enticing to me. I shared that description with Linda, and she was on board for our adventure trek.

The base of the mountain where the trek begins is about two and a half hours from Tokyo, so we decided to meet at the Tokyo bus station the next morning. The bus took us to station 5 (7,562 feet) to begin our climb. On our bus was a young Japanese woman and her tiny, wizened grandmother, also going to station 5. *How nice* I thought. *Probably a grandmother/granddaughter sightseeing trip.* As we parted at the bus stop, they bowed and said something in Japanese and we bowed and said, "Have a good day."

Before I continue, I must make a confession. As you might expect, we were ill prepared once again for the challenges ahead. We had the good sense to wear blue jeans but were soon to discover our planning shortfall. I wore a sweater, windbreaker, and a pair of sneakers. With our water bottles in hand, we began our climb up the mountainside. In some areas, the trail was almost straight up. Because of the light drizzle earlier in the day, the rocks were wet and slippery. It would be all too easy to lose our footing. For Linda and me, who lived at sea level, the higher the altitude the more labored our breathing became. Linda, I discovered, was a smoker, which made her gasp for breath. As we climbed, I thought several times that perhaps we should turn back, but we weren't quitters. Periodically, men with heavy packs of supplies on their backs would run past us up the mountain to the huts at stations up the mountain. We kept on trekking.

It was getting very dark about 8:00 p.m. when we finally stopped at station 8, to have dinner and spend the night. Except for a few crackers and our water, we had not eaten since breakfast. We each ate a large bowl of Japanese noodle soup which tasted better than any noodle soup I had ever eaten.

As to the sleeping accommodations, they were primitive at best. There were two sleeping rooms, each with two bunk beds and no door. Much to my surprise, we were the only women spending the night. We were stiff, tired, and cold and had no other choice. The bathroom was an outhouse literally out on the slope. We were each given one small wool blanket. After some discussion, we decided for warmth and safety's sake, we would sleep together in the top bunk bed. The guide book said that the sun rose about 4:30 a.m. on the mountain and, of course, we wanted to see the "mystical sight" so we got up at 3:00 a.m. and began climbing the final 2,200 feet in near darkness. By now, the altitude was greatly affecting both of us. My oxygen-deprived legs throbbed constantly. I was climbing short distances and then stopping to suck in oxygen, wondering when we would ever get to the top.

The sun did rise that morning but we didn't see it. The top of Mt. Fuji was covered in a dense cloud cover. It made me smile, thinking of the old adage "The best laid plans of mice and men..."

Coming down the opposite side of the mountain presented a new challenge. There was still an abundance of snow left from winter storms. We had to walk through that snow to get down to base camp. Our sneakers were soaked as we walked. You would have thought we had climbed Mt. Everest. "There's no turning back now!" I exclaimed as I took my first steps into the snow and sank in up to my thighs. It was wet, slushy snow, so now my sneakers and my pant legs were wet. As I struggled to take additional steps down the mountain, guess who should come along? The Japanese grandmother and her granddaughter! They were wearing snowshoes! As they practically skied by us, the grandmother turned and bowed in our direction. I hollered "Good morning to you," but could not have bowed to save my life. By the time Linda and I sloshed our way to the bottom of the mountain, they were sitting under a tree finishing their picnic lunch and thermos of tea.

Reflections

I spent two more nights with the Nakasones before heading off to Kyoto, Nara, and Osaka. They were kind, thoughtful hosts. When I told Mr. Nakasone I was going to Hong Kong in a week, he told me that Mieko's older sister, Michiko, was studying in Hong Kong for the summer, and that I must call her when I arrived in Hong Kong. She would be awaiting my call.

How amazing it was to realize that 21 years before we had just ended the Second World War. The Japanese had bombed Pearl Harbor, and we had dropped atomic bombs on Hiroshima and Nagasaki. In a relatively short time, the United States and Japan had come a long way towards healing those wounds. Here I was in Japan being treated like an honored guest not only by the Nakasones but by people I met on the street who helped me with directions, translated, and even travelled with me briefly. I wondered to myself if the proverbial shoe were on the other foot and we Americans had lost the war, would we have been so gracious?

One evening, 16 years later in 1982, I was watching the nightly newscaster who was announcing the results of the Japanese election and introducing the newly elected prime minister of Japan, Yasuhiro Nakasone. I couldn't believe my eyes! Despite a slight graying around his temples and a western style business suit, it was indeed my host and friend Mr. Nakasone.

港 香 角叁圓壹

HONG KONG $1·30

Hong Kong Moving On

I was relieved when my ship docked in Hong Kong after a four-day cruise from Yokohama. I was grateful that I would be flying the remaining legs of my journey.

The pier in Hong Kong Harbor was awash with people who had come to meet friends and family. At the end of the pier, cars, taxis, and rickshaws vied for riders. As I edged my way down the pier through the throngs of people, the sky looked increasingly ominous. Large gray thunder clouds loomed overhead. *It's going to pour* I thought as I quickened my pace. The wind was blowing strongly now and the rain was beginning to fall. I quickly stepped under an overhang to avoid getting drenched. It rained cats and dogs. Then, as suddenly as it started, the rain stopped, the sun came out, creating a beautiful rainbow.

Since I had the address of the student hostel in downtown Hong Kong, but had no city map, I hired a little local man, not much bigger than myself, to take me there in his bicycle-driven rickshaw. As we wended our way in and out of traffic, I got my first bird's eye view of the city. I was surprised to find Hong Kong much hillier than I expected. The city seemed like a hodge-podge of old and new: large and small businesses, high rises, and expensive homes just yards away from tenements on the hillside. Here and there I saw signs of western culture, like the very large red and white Coca Cola sign hanging on a storefront window.

That first afternoon, I called Michiko Nakasone because I had promised her father I would do so. She was expecting my phone call. We decided to meet the next day at a very ornate cemetery not too far from my hostel. Michiko added that her father had arranged with two Japanese business associates currently living in Hong Kong to escort us to dinner afterward.

The next afternoon, with map in hand, I began my trek to meet Michiko. It appeared that the shortest distance to the cemetery was over the hill, not around it. What I didn't know initially was that footpath wound its way through the tenements so precariously perched on the hillside. It was hot and muggy after a rain shower, which seemed to be a daily occurrence. Barefoot, partially clothed Chinese children waded in dirty puddles of rain water. A little girl was rinsing out several chipped tea cups at a communal water pipe, which seemed to be the only clean water source. The tenements were very simple cardboard and wire buildings with scrap metal roofs. Some of the children were as curious about me as I was about them, and they followed me at a distance before turning back to home.

When I finally got to the top of the hill, I could see the cemetery with its idols and statues far below. Much to my surprise, it was fenced in-probably to protect it from vandals. There below at the entrance was a little Japanese woman. "Yoo Hoo" I called down to her to assure her I was on my way.

Michiko was definitely Mieko's sister. She, too, had taken English lessons but, understandably, Mieko's speech was much clearer having lived in the United States for a year. I frankly remember very little about the cemetery. We did talk a lot about her family and Mieko and

Mieko's transition home.

That evening, about 6:00 p.m., two Japanese businessmen in suits and ties picked us up and drove us to one of the elegant paddle boat restaurants permanently moored in the river. As we approached the brightly lit boat, the doormen opened the restaurant door. The flood of light from the chandeliers made a pathway for us to enter. The table settings were pristine: gold table clothes, cloth napkins, silverware, chopsticks, water and wine goblets. I immediately realized that I was significantly under-dressed in my wrinkled skirt and blouse pulled from the bottom of my backpack.

Our escorts did all the ordering, which was fine with me. We had more gourmet dishes than we could possibly eat, the most memorable being a whole lobster. Secretly, I wished I could have packed up the leftovers and taken them to the children I had seen earlier that day.

I thanked our escorts and asked Michiko to please thank her father for the wonderful evening. Since Michiko had classes the next day, we had to say goodbye. It was great fun meeting her. After all these years I still have a very warm feeling in my heart for the Japanese people.

On My Own–Another Life Lesson

The next afternoon, I was walking around an upscale indoor mall looking for a restaurant to have a late lunch or early dinner. As I stood attempting to read the mall directory, a young man approached me. "May I help you," he asked with a rather thick Chinese accent. (I had been approached many times by young men in Japan all saying that they wanted to practice their English with me, so this was nothing new.) I explained that I was looking for a place to eat a late lunch. He said he, too, was looking for a restaurant for lunch.

He asked if I had ever eaten dim sum, the Chinese version of Spanish tapas. He suggested that we go together, and he would translate for me. A nice gesture. I looked more closely at this young man. He was wearing a long sleeved white dress shirt and black slacks, which seemed to be the standard garb of university students both in Japan and Hong Kong. He was very polite and well spoken. Yes, we could eat dim sum together.

At the end of the meal, he insisted on paying for my lunch, saying that I was his guest. As we walked out of the restaurant, he asked me what my plans were for the rest of the afternoon. I had no definite plans. He suggested that we take the ferry to Macao which was about 65 kilometers from Hong Kong. Why not?

It took much longer to get there than I anticipated, so it was late afternoon when we arrived. To my surprise, Macao was a gambling mecca. Well-dressed people were placing large bets at roulette and black jack tables. Chinese hostesses were delivering drink orders. Lots of money was changing hands. We sat and people watched for a while. It was dusk and I was anxious to return to the ferry and head for Hong Kong.

My escort had other plans. "I have a friend who lives in one of the high rises and would like to stop and say hello before we go back to the ferry," he said. Against my better judgment, I agreed. We took the elevator to the eighth floor and knocked several times. "He's not here," I said. "I'm going back to the ferry." I was feeling very vulnerable at this point. Not good, I realized.

He pulled a key from his pocket, opened the door, and stepped inside. It was a one bedroom apartment with a spectacular view of the harbor. It was very sparsely furnished as though no one lived there with two small chairs in the front room and a small cot in the corner of the bedroom. That was all. My heart was pounding.

"Since my friend is not here, we can spend the night and return in the morning."

"I'm not staying," I blurted out.

"It is dangerous for a woman to be on the street alone at night," he countered.

I looked him straight in the eye. "It is dangerous for me to stay in this apartment," I retorted. Despite our cultural and language differences, we understood each other completely.

"I'll take my chances on the street," I announced as I walked towards the door. Abruptly, he stepped in front of me. He paused for a long moment. I wished I was a mind reader. Well, maybe not. Then he said, "You can have the bedroom. It has a lock on the inside. You will be safe."

It was very dark outside now. I asked myself, "Do I choose the devil that I know or the devil that I don't know?" I considered the bedroom one more time. There was, in fact, a dead bolt on the door. The decision was made.

I lay awake a long time pondering what had happened and very grateful that I was safe. What did I say or do that prompted his actions, or was this the plan all along? One thing I promised the Lord and myself: From now on, I would be much more careful about picking up with young men who approached me and would stop assuming they were only interested in practicing their English!

BANGKOK

THAILAND

Shall We Dance?

My next stop was Bangkok, Thailand. I must admit that I had a romantic notion about Thailand based solely on the movie *The King and I*. When I closed my eyes, I could picture the handsome, bald-headed, bronze-skinned Yul Brenner, King of Siam, learning to dance with petite, charming Deborah Kerr, a romantic scene that made my heart flutter. As you might guess, my Bangkok experience was nothing like the movie.

By this point in my trip, I had been gone for more than a month. Some days it felt much longer than that. I was homesick for Mike and my family. My parents were preparing to spend the month of August at the family cottage in Canada, and I was more than halfway around the world.

I took a big breath as I stepped off the airplane in Bangkok, gathered up my backpack and entered the terminal. My first need was a map of Bangkok and directions to the student youth hostel. The first office I came to was Air France. A little woman in her 40s wearing a neatly-pressed Air France uniform greeted me at the counter. I asked for a city map of Bangkok.

"Where do you wish to go?" she asked.

"I'm looking for the student youth hostel," I explained.

She began speaking to the other Air France agent in Thai as she rummaged through the desk. Finally, she pulled out a map. She pointed to the area of the city where the hostel was located and shook her head. "You cannot stay there. It is not safe."

Where had I heard that before?

"How long will you be in Bangkok?" she asked. I told her I would be there three nights. Her next comment really surprised me. "You can stay with my two daughters and me."

For a moment, I was speechless. "But you don't know me," I mumbled.

She was very insistent. I could ride home with her in her little car when she finished her work shift. I must say that I was rather ambivalent about her invitation. On the one hand, it would be interesting to meet her family and spend time in a Thai home. On the other, I felt uneasy about the invitation from a stranger. What was she thinking?

My Thai hostess was a single parent with two young daughters at home. I wondered if she was widowed or divorced, but I never got a clear answer. Her husband was simply gone. There was an adult male in the home during the evenings whom she introduced as her friend.

The home was small with two bedrooms and the inside was rather dark. Dinners were simple: rice or noodles with various vegetables, sauce and occasionally some chicken or fish. We ate on the floor at short tables. At the end of the meal, we washed the dishes on a little concrete pad on the ground behind the house. The dishes were turned upside down and left on the pad to air dry. In hindsight, I am surprised that I didn't get dysentery.

The twelve-year-old daughter had taken a little English in school. She followed me around like a puppy, practicing her English.

During the day, when the family was at work and school, I ventured out with my map to see more of Bangkok. One of my favorite tours was the canal tour to see the floating market. Vendors in their little wooden boats, chock full of produce, bought and sold colorful fruits and vegetables, flowers rice and noodles, tea, and seasonings.

On my last evening, my hostess said she had arranged a special surprise for me. She took me to a classical Thai dance program held in one of the luxury hotels. Unlike the other guests, we entered through the back door, and were greeted by her friend, who ushered us quickly to our seats. I noticed the sign for the tickets was $15. That was a lot of money, so I offered to reimburse her for my ticket. She refused, saying that her friend had made special arrangements. The classical dancers wore elaborate gold gilded costumes and heavy make-up reminding me once again of a scene from the *King and I*.

It was kind and thoughtful of my hostess to take me to the performance concert. I told her so as she drove me to the international airport to catch my plane to Calcutta the next day. As I was thanking her again for her hospitality, she said, "I have a request. When you return to the United States, please ask your parents to adopt my twelve-year-old daughter. I do not want to keep her in Bangkok. It is not a good place to raise girls."

I stiffened. I reminded her that I was from a large family and was doubtful that my parents had the space, money, or energy to raise another child. She stared at me. "I have treated you like family for three days in my home. You owe me the respect of asking your parents about adopting my daughter." I nodded as she turned and disappeared in the Air France office. In hindsight, if I had not been so startled by her request, I would have asked the obvious question: *Why are you so fearful for your daughter's safety?* It left me with mixed feelings about our encounter.

Calcutta

I flew from Bangkok to Calcutta for the sole purpose of catching a flight to Kathmandu, Nepal. My flight arrived late afternoon, so it was impossible to make a connecting flight. True to its promise, the airline arranged with a hotel in central Calcutta for my overnight stay. Much to my surprise, it was a lovely old Colonial style hotel with oriental rugs, wicker furniture, and leather easy chairs in the lobby. According to my travel voucher, my flight to Kathmandu took off at 6:00 a.m. I was to report to the Nepalese airline ticket office at 4:00 a.m. I would have to take a cab around 3:45 a.m. to be there on time. The desk clerk, a gentleman wearing a turban, assured me that the doorman would hail me a taxi at that time of night.

As planned, I was in the lobby very early the next morning. As I walked out the door, I was faced with a sea of male bodies sleeping on the concrete under the hotel portico. The door man whistled for a taxi, and then moved the men aside, making a path for me to walk. Fortunately, the taxi driver spoke a little English. We sped off through the dark streets of Calcutta to the airline office. The Nepalese Airlines did have a light on, and other passengers had begun to gather to be processed. Among them was an American couple with four children, each dressed in matching shirts and black backpacks. While we were waiting, we struck up a conversation. The parents were teachers who had taught in Germany in the Department of Defense school. Now they were taking some side trips on their way home so that the children could see other countries and customs of the world. "What an interesting idea!" I thought. "Travel is a part of one's education."

The airline representative called my name. He needed both my passport and my visa in order to process me and give me a seat assignment. "What visa?" I asked.

"The visa from the Nepalese consulate," he replied.

"I don't have a visa. Can't I just buy one from you?"

"Sorry, Miss," he said. "You must go to the consulate during working hours and get your visa. I will rebook you on tomorrow's flight to Kathmandu."

It was 4:30 a.m. – I was tired and at a loss. What to do? I decided that the best thing was to retrace my steps and return to the hotel. I knew that the airline was paying for my room for one night but now I would have to pay for me own lodging. Also, I knew I couldn't afford to pay for another night in this elegant old hotel room with its own private bath.

The same gentlemen from the previous night was behind the desk. "You have returned," he acknowledged.

I explained my dilemma. Needed a visa…flight rebooked for tomorrow, very limited funds.

He said in a kind and fatherly sounding voice, "You are very tired. Go back to bed for a few hours and have breakfast. We will talk about this then."

I didn't need to be told twice. I climbed into my bed with all my clothes on, pulled the duvet cover over me, and slept soundly. The next time I looked at my watch it was 9:00 a.m. I went downstairs and had a sumptuous breakfast of porridge, eggs, bangers, toast with marmalade, and a pot of English tea.

It was time to get mobilized and go to the Nepalese consulate. I spoke again to the desk clerk. He gave me directions via the trolley car and said that the conductor would signal me at the correct stop. "And," he added, "about your room. I have been able to arrange it so that you are our guest for an additional night."

I swallowed hard trying to thank him without crying. Another blessing.

Getting to the Nepalese consulate sounded simple enough. The trolley originated in the park less than a block away from my hotel. It was almost empty when I boarded. I took a seat by the window so I could watch the scenery going by: Children begging, street dogs sniffing through garbage, a man urinating on the side of a building. The trolley was becoming more and more crowded with each stop. I saw one man, desperate to board the trolley, put his foot in the back of the person in front of him and shove him onto the trolley car. We were packed in like sardines with standing room only. How was I going to get off the trolley at my stop?

When the conductor signaled me, I managed to stand up and face the wall of people that encapsulated me. Suddenly, from nowhere (or so it seemed), a tall, middle-aged gentleman with a neatly trimmed beard said, "Follow me!" I obeyed his instructions. I kept my eyes on his turban as he parted the crowd with his long arms, just as Moses parted the Red Sea. He maneuvered our way off the trolley and led me down a side street to the Nepalese consulate. I was so grateful. I'd still be entombed if it were not for him. When I thanked him, he bowed and disappeared around the corner.

After some wait, I was able to get my visa and catch the trolley back to the park. It was beginning to rain when I stepped off the trolley. As I hurried for shelter, I noticed a severely crippled beggar with mangled legs and deformed feet sitting in the dirt. He was desperately trying to inch his way to shelter, too. I was troubled as I watched people walk or run by him. The dirt was rapidly becoming mud. Here was this crippled man with mud on his clothing, rain- matted hair, soaked to the skin, and no hope that anyone would help him..

He didn't weigh much more than me, I surmised. *Maybe I could pull him to shelter.* I knew he was dead weight. I needed help. I ran across the street to my hotel doorman and explained the problem. This man needed help.

The doorman slowly shook his head and said, "No, **Memsaab** . Do not touch him." This was my first experience with the Hindu caste and untouchables system in India.[1] *Why did people more fortunate ignore and neglect them? What happened to "Do unto others…"* Then it came to me. *Don't we in the United States treat the homeless in much the same way?* When I could bear the sight no longer, I stepped inside the hotel into a different world. It was time for tea.

---

1 The castes were divided into four official groups: the Brahmane (priestly order); followed by the rulers and warriors; then the artisans, merchants, and farmers; and finally the laborers. The untouchables were the lowest – not even meriting an official caste. They were not allowed in the temple and were assigned the dirtiest jobs such as preparing corpses for cremation. Many were beggars.

KATHMANDU

NEPAL

Kathmandu, Nepal–
On the Road Again

I watched the sunrise over the Himalayas from the window of the airplane. The snow-covered peaks sparkled like diamonds in the early morning sunshine. These magnificent mountains dwarfed Mt. Fuji, which was approximately one third their height.

Upon landing midmorning in the Kathmandu valley, I decided that I needed to locate the student youth hostel. I wanted to reserve a cot for the night and to stow my backpack, which was getting heavier by the day.

The youth hostel was housed in an old estate home. It had cavernous walls, old oriental rugs, stone floors, and a very strong musty odor. The female sleeping quarters was a large room jammed with cots. I could barely squeeze between them. I just hoped that nobody snored or needed to get to the bathroom in the middle of the night.

Speaking of the bathroom, there was one small bathroom for the females. The toilet was a hole in the floor with two places on either side to put one's feet. I presumed that unless I was an excellent marksman, I was supposed to squat. I nicknamed it "The Turkish Bomb Shelter."

I was told to claim a cot, and to put my backpack on the foot of my bed. That was somewhat of a surprise since other hostels had locked up the luggage providing safe keeping during the day.

Since the hostel did not officially open until 5:00 p.m., I decided to walk into town. The first thing I noticed was the large number of cattle roaming through the city streets and on sidewalks. Several cattle walked into a home.

What is this? I asked myself. I knew that many Hindus were vegetarians, but it seemed strange to see cattle treated like family pets. A young Nepali university student explained that cattle were sacred in Nepal. In fact, many housewives put out scraps of leftovers for the cattle much like Americans set out scraps for their family dogs.

The second thing I noticed was the many wires strung between buildings: phone wires, electrical wires, clothes lines, and who knows what else, spun in intricate spider like webs.

When I returned to the hostel in the late afternoon, I immediately sensed something was wrong. My backpack had been moved, and several of the clasps were open. The contents looked as though it had been dumped out, rummaged through and jammed back into the bag. Worst of all, the souvenirs for Mike and my family, which I had so ardently bargained for at the street market in Bangkok, were missing. Silver bracelets, a silk scarf, and several silk ties were all gone. All in all, I had spent more than $40.

For me, in 1966, that was a lot of money. I tried to question the young matron who had checked me in that morning. She spoke very little English. I was getting very frustrated. I felt violated. Sensing my frustration, she led me to the hostel manager's sitting room on the other side of the old estate home. In a few minutes, the hostel manager appeared dressed in a suit jacket despite the heat. The matron began speaking to him in her native tongue. He then turned to me and asked "How may I help you?"

I explained that while the hostel was closed during the day, my backpack had been ransacked and I had been robbed.

He again spoke to the matron. "No," she said. She had not taken anything. After about ten minutes of back and forth, I was not only getting frustrated but also angry.

"If we cannot get this resolved peacefully, I will go to the American consulate with my complaint." He told me that he wanted to speak with his staff and would get back with me. He was now listening more attentively.

After supper, I was summoned to the manager's sitting room once again. There on a table were several of my souvenirs from my backpack. When I pointed out that these were only part of my belongings, he simply shrugged as if to say, "Be grateful that you got some of your belongings back."

I must admit that being robbed was very disconcerting. I did not feel safe in this third- world country, so I cut my visit to Nepal short staying just one more night and returned to India with a new life lesson that I would soon not forget. These poor people didn't feel it a crime to take from the rich tourists. *Hang on to your important things!*

Back to India

India is a very big country. I knew that I would only have a handful of days to sightsee, so I picked my sights carefully. I decided to fly to the town of Benares (also known as Varanasi) along the Ganges River. This was the holy place where the Hindus cremated their dead. I stayed at a youth hostel that was six or seven miles away from Varanasi.

I felt a sense of inner peace and personal safety in India that I had not felt in Nepal. Dinner that night was curried lentils, rice, and a piece of wonderfully warm flat bread called naan. I also met some fellow hostellers who were planning to go to the Ganges to see the funeral pyres in the morning. One young Indian man asked if I would like to share the cost of a bicycle-driven rickshaw in the morning. His offer sounded like a good idea to me.

After breakfast the following morning, we negotiated a fare with a rickshaw driver. He said it would cost the equivalent of 16¢ apiece to take us there. It was a gray, sultry morning. and perspiration dripped from the driver's brow. In the end, I gave him 50¢ for his efforts. My tip made him very happy, and the fare was still an enormous bargain for us.

When we reached the ghats (a series of steps leading down to a body of water, particularly a holy river), our driver motioned to us to disembark.

While I was standing there a bit overwhelmed by the crowds and funeral pyres, a priest in his clerical collar approached us. He looked to be in his late 50s. He had white hair and black-rimmed glasses. He explained that he was an ordained Episcopalian priest. Since his church parish was very poor, he supplemented his income by leading guided tours. He had a very old wooden row boat that would hold four people. He would take us out on the river for a bird's eye view of the cremation ceremonies for $5.00 each. That seemed like an interesting and reasonable thing to do. I accepted his offer, as did two other travelers.

The first place he took us was to a Hindu Temple near the river. I dubbed it the *Monkey Temple*. Hindus prepared trays of fruit for the monkeys, and took them down to the temple. There were monkeys everywhere, fighting over food, throwing peels on the floor, and defecating. How could this be a holy place? The stench was indescribable.

As we walked away from the temple through a covered walkway, I noticed there were beggars in the shadows, sitting on the ground along the pathways. As my eyes became more acclimated to the low light, I realized that several of the beggars had part of their noses and/or cheeks missing. One man was trying to cover his face to prevent the ever-present flies from entering the wound. "So this is what leprosy looks like," I thought to myself. "How very sad it is!"

Our tour guide was talking as we walked toward the river. He pointed to a Planned Parenthood poster on a bulletin board. The family on the left was a well-dressed Indian couple with two children, a boy and a girl. On the right side of the poster was a much larger Indian family with disheveled clothing. Some of them were without shoes. "The poster is supposed to convince Indian families to use birth control." Our guide added. "Instead, the poorer families look at the poster, shake their heads and say, "How unfortunate it is that this family has only two children."

We rowed very quietly to the middle of the river to watch the cremations. Bodies wrapped in linen cloth were carried on bamboo stretchers to the funeral pyres. Sometimes the bodies were dipped into the Ganges. Other times, water was sprinkled over the body. Wood was then placed around, under, and on top of the cadaver, and a flammable liquid was poured over it. It ignited like an explosion – ashes to ashes.

Meanwhile, just a short distance down river, pilgrims who had come to this holy site were bathing, brushing their teeth, and washing their clothes in this amazingly dirty water.

On to New Delhi

I flew from Benares to New Delhi. For a change of pace, I decided to treat myself to a one night stay in an old, charming bed and breakfast in the countryside. It had a lovely, serene outdoor patio where breakfast was served. My plan for the day was to find public transportation, probably a local bus to Agra, the site of the Taj Mahal. It was a significant distance from New Delhi on my map.

As I was sitting on the patio, sipping breakfast tea, and planning my long day ahead, a distinguished looking, gray haired gentleman in a business suit and a much younger man sat down at a garden table near me. I could tell they were Germans from their accents. They struck up a conversation with me. The older gentleman was the CEO of a successful German company. His company did business with several Indian firms. Since the senior statesman was about to retire, he had planned this trip to introduce his son to his Indian business contacts and to say good bye in person. That seemed like a kind and thoughtful gesture on his part.

As I got up from the breakfast table, the senior statesman asked how I planned to spend my day. He said that they were going sightseeing to the Taj Mahal in Agra. They had rented a car and driver to drive them there. Would I be interested in going with them? He said that the Taj Mahal was approximately 125 miles from Delhi, too far to go on a public bus in one day. I appreciated his kind invitation.

It was a long and bumpy ride to Agra, even in an air-conditioned luxury car. We traveled through one village after another: stray dogs, babies on mothers' backs, hovels, dirty clothing, and always lots of flies.

The Taj Mahal's history was very interesting. Emperor Shah Jahan built it as a tribute to his favorite wife who died in child birth delivering their thirteenth child. Construction of the monument began in 1632. It took 17 years and approximately 20,000 laborers to complete.

As we approached it, I could see the reflection of Taj's marble onion-shaped dome in a pool at the foot of the monument. It was a beautiful tribute to his wife and lover. Outside the carefully guarded compound, I saw a lone Indian woman sitting on the wet cobblestone street next to a young baby...flies everywhere. So many incidents on this trip had shown me the very poor people living in the shadow of the very rich. I asked myself, *What would have happened if that emperor had spent the money and resources that he used to build the Taj Mahal to build schools, to educate the poor, and feed the starving population of India. Wouldn't that have more greatly honored his deceased wife?*

Baghdad-Damacus-Jerusalem-Tel Aviv-London-Toronto-Illinois

I was rounding third base, and heading for home plate, figuratively speaking. I flew from India to Baghdad, Iraq, for no other reason than to see a Middle Eastern Arab city.

My notable memories of Baghdad are few. It was a tiny city sitting in the desert on an ocean of sand. Despite the fact that it was an overcast day, I had never been so hot in all my life! If I was reading the thermometer correctly, it was well over 115 degrees mid-day. I was drinking everything in sight to stay hydrated.

My last memory of Baghdad was standing on the tarmac at the airport about noon the next day waiting to board my airplane. Next to me were four or five women clothed head to toe in black burqas with veils covering their faces. I couldn't understand how or why they could do that in the smothering heat.

Time to move on!

Damascus, Syria was my next stop. My most vivid memory is

walking into the city on an unpaved country road behind an old wooden ox cart loaded with hay. I imagined Paul on the road to Damascus almost 2,000 years before on a similar summer afternoon being struck blind by the Lord. It was a *Come to Jesus* moment.

Israel was my final stop on my self-led journey around the world. By this point in my trip, I was tired, missing Mike, and my family. I must admit that I was very tempted to cancel my Israel stop-over and just go home. However, the more practical side of me realized that this might be the only opportunity in my life to visit the Holy Land and it would be a mistake not to *seize the day*.

I flew to Jerusalem. I loved the old walled city and I meandered through the market place listening to shopkeepers and customers bargaining with one another. At the Wailing Wall, I wrote my prayer request for "Peace on Earth" and wedged it into a crevice in the wall. I've been praying that same prayer ever since.

My final destination was the Church of the Nativity in Bethlehem, the site where Jesus was born. I was surprised and dismayed to find that the church had been subdivided into three different Christian groups: Greek Orthodox, Armenian Orthodox, and the Franciscan order of monks. Each group was soliciting donations. Needless to say, it detracted from the religious experience.

When I flew to Tel Aviv I could not make my plane connection to London. Again the airline was true to its word. It arranged for a very nice hotel room for me at its expense in a meticulously kept high rise with a view of the city.

I altered my airline ticket one last time. I decided to fly to Toronto instead of Chicago, since I was ending my trip approximately ten days early. My roommates and I could not move into our apartment until September first. Also, Mike was living with his parents in Lockport, Illinois and working two jobs to earn enough money to return to medical school in September. My family was in Ontario at our summer cottage, and my parents had just celebrated their 25th wedding anniversary. I wanted to be there.

"That settles it, then," I thought. "I'm going to Canada." Much to my surprise and delight, the airline ticket agent handed me a check for $95 explaining that the plane ticket to Toronto was cheaper than the ticket to Chicago. I arrived in Toronto on a Saturday afternoon, and discovered that the milk train made a red-eye run to Parry Sound, Ontario, that night. I knew that if I could get to Parry Sound, I could get a boat ride the 27 miles to my parents' cottage in Woods Bay.

On that slow overnight train trip, I hatched an even better plan. Why not walk over to Georgian Bay Airways in Parry Sound and see if I could get a ride on the pontoon plane that delivered the mail.

One problem: It was early Sunday morning and the office was closed. I did see a phone number on the door and called. Much to my surprise, thirty minutes later I was boarding the single engine pontoon plane, and we were scooting across the open bay. Soon we were flying above the tree line, looking down on the majestic blue waters of Georgian Bay.

The reality of my long around the world sojourn was sinking in. I had learned so many valuable lessons on this trip about racial prejudice, the plight of the poor, the low status of women and children, and a variety of cultural differences, as well as human kindness. How blessed I was to live in the United States.

I took a deep cleansing breath. I pointed to the island just off to our left. The pilot nodded and prepared to land. As we taxied up to our boat dock, I could see several of my younger siblings running towards the plane. As I emerged from the plane, my sister Judith shrieked as if she had seen a ghost. "It's Frances! She's come home."

I had taken a trip to discover the world and in the process, found myself as well.

Epilogue - 2017

Yes, I did marry Mike in September 1967. So, this year we will celebrate our 50th wedding anniversary. Mike became a Family Medicine physician and I graduated with a Master's degree in clinical social work. Mike joined the Air Force after his residency and we were fortunate to be stationed in Athens, Greece. That is a story for another time. Mike and I have three very special adult children who are married and have blessed us with wonderful grandchildren.

My around-the-world trip changed the way I saw life. My adventures put me on an unanticipated career path. Being married to Mike has been an interesting 50 years, ranging from private practice to working for hospice to a high risk counselor at a high school in Charlottesville Virginia to a consultant for a nursing home.

Both Mike and I are retired now. In addition to writing my stories, I volunteer for our church's Stephen's ministry--a Christian caring ministry. After our time in Greece, Mike started a private small town practice, then joined the Department of Family Medicine at University of Virginia where he became the Vice Chairman, and finally became the Chairman of the Department of Family Medicine at University of Oklahoma. Now, in his retirement, he is very active in our church where he is a Deacon of Missions.

I hope that this story has blessed you and encouraged you. Our adventures have enriched our lives and we pray that all of us will....

.....*bear one another's burdens, and in this way you will fulfill the law of Christ (Galatians 6:2, NRSV)*

About the Author

Francie Morse was born in 1943 during World War II. As the oldest of six children, she quickly became her mother's helper. The Women's Liberation Movement was underway. Women had earned the right to vote, and were exercising that right in record numbers. More women were working outside the home. The times were in turmoil.

Francie's mother was a *closet feminist*—keeping the home fires burning but also involved in women's issues such as *The League of Women's Voters*, writing a weekly column for the local newspaper and organizing the first women's investment club in her town. When her youngest child began school, she returned to college and graduated with a bachelor's degree in social psychology. Needless to say, Francie was greatly influenced by her role model.

Francie attended Knox College in Galesburg, Illinois, majoring in English literature. Her father was more practical and insisted she also get her teaching certification so that she get gainful employment after graduation. Francie believed that life offered women a smörgåsbord of interesting opportunities including foreign travel. Therefore, it should not have surprised her parents when she announced that she was ready to strike out on her own to see the world. No one could have imagined what was about to happen to a single 22 year old female with less than $200 in her pocket as she boarded a train in Kansas City heading west.

We invite you to come along on this very interesting life changing journey.

Francie Morse is a retired licensed clinical social worker. She and her husband Mike will celebrate their 50th wedding anniversary in September. They have three adult children and six grandchildren.

Made in the USA
Middletown, DE
18 September 2017